CHEMISTRY IN THE KITCHEN

CHEMISTRY IN THE KITCHEN

Beverly Le Blanc

CHERRY TREE BOOKS

A Cherrytree Book

Designed and produced by
Pemberton Press Ltd

First published 1992
by Cherrytree Press Ltd
a subsidiary of
The Chivers Company Ltd
Windsor Bridge Road
Bath, Avon BA2 3AX

Copyright © Cherrytree Press Ltd 1992

British Library Cataloguing in Publication Data

Le Blanc, Beverly
  Chemistry in the Kitchen
  1. Chemistry
  I. Title II. Series
  540

  ISBN 0-7451-5118-3

Contents

Kitchen Chemistry

Freezing   8
Floating Ice   10
Melting   11
Boiling   12
Cooking by Boiling   13
Dissolving   14
Filtering   15
Suspensions   16
Mixing Oil and Vinegar   17
Carbon Dioxide   18
Carbon Dioxide in Action   19
Starches   20
Enzymes   21
Acids at Work   22
Vitamin C   23
Hard and Soft Water   24
Salt Water   25
Ethylene Gas   26
Pretty Flowers   27
Searching for Light   28
Healthy Eating   30
Making Bread   34
Flourless Baking   38
Juicy Kebabs   39
Moulds in the Air   40
Making Glue   41

Safety Notes   42
Words to Remember   44
Books to Read   46
Index   47

Getting Started

Before you do any experiments, take a few minutes to read the Safety Notes on page 42 at the back of the book. None of these experiments is dangerous, but you will need to be careful in handling some of the household items. If you read something that is not clear to you, or if you have any questions about an experiment, ask an adult or an older friend for some help.

Some of the experiments have a marker that looks like this:

This means that you should ask permission to do the experiment. You may need help from an adult.

DO NOT do experiments marked

unless an adult is available to help you.

In all of the experiments, try to follow the directions as closely as possible. For the experiments in which you need to make something, the drawings will help you understand more about the things you are building. Most of the experiments will work better if you follow the drawings as closely as you can. If an experiment doesn't work first time, try to work out why and then try again.

Kitchen Chemistry

Chemistry is the science of the way different substances are made and how they can be changed. Most chemists work in laboratories. Your house probably has a built-in lab where you can study chemistry – in the kitchen.

Almost all cookery uses chemistry or chemical processes. When you boil water, you change the water from a liquid into a gas. You also change the composition of any food you cook in it.

All the experiments in this book show at least one chemical process. Several of them also produce a delicious result.

Freezing

Freezing is what happens when a liquid turns to a solid. The molecules in the solid stick together and do not move. Ice is frozen water. Water freezes at 0°C (32°F). This is called the "freezing point". When water turns to ice it expands. This means it takes up more space.

"Growing" water

Here are two experiments that show how water expands when it freezes.

You will need
a plastic cup
water
a pencil

1. Fill a plastic cup half full of water.

2. Use a pencil to mark the water level on the side of the cup. Put the cup in the freezer until ice forms.

Where is the top of the ice? It should be above the pencil mark because ice takes up more space than water. Mark the new level.

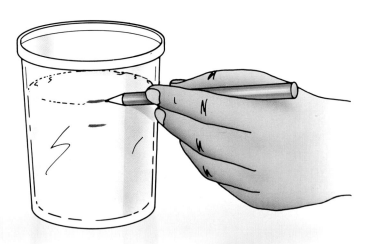

1. Fill a plastic cup to the brim with water.

2. Place a piece of cling film over the top of the cup so it lies flat. Use a rubber band to hold the cling film in place. Put the cup in the freezer until ice forms.

You will need
a plastic cup
water
cling film
a rubber band

Has the ice pushed up the cling film? The cling film should be bulging because ice takes up more space than water.

Floating Ice

All ice floats even if it is as small as an ice cube. Most of the ice floats under the water like an iceberg.

Only about one-tenth of an iceberg is above the water level. The water expanded this much while it was freezing. Ice floats because it is not as dense as water and therefore weighs less.

Making an iceberg

You can make your own iceberg to float in a bowl of water.

You will need

a plastic cup
water
food colouring (optional)
a clear bowl

1. Fill a plastic cup with water. Stir in a drop of food colouring. The colouring will make it easier for you to see the ice float.

2. Put the cup in the freezer for several hours until the water turns to ice.

3. Remove the cup from the freezer. Hold the cup under warm running water in the sink, then remove the ice.

4. Fill a glass bowl with water. Put the coloured ice into the water.

How much of the ice is under water? Does the ice sink or float? You should be able to see that most of the ice floats under the water's surface.

Did You Know?

Have you ever heard people use the expression "the tip of the iceberg"? It is a way of saying that only a small amount of information is known about a situation, just like an iceberg, where only the tip can be seen.

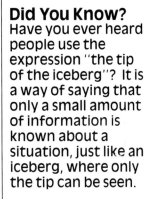

Melting

Melting is what happens when a solid turns to liquid. The molecules in a liquid do not remain in one position. This is why liquids flow and can be splashed. If ice melts, it turns back to water. The melting point is 0°C (32°F). This is the same as the freezing point. If the temperature moves a fraction above 0°C (32°F), the ice will start to melt.

Turning ice to water

1. Make two plastic cups of ice. Mark the level of the ice.

2. Melt one cup of ice at room temperature.

3. Melt the other in the refrigerator.

Which cup of ice melts first? It should be the one at room temperature. This is because the warmer the temperature, the faster ice melts.

When the ice has melted, where is the water level? It should be below the pencil level. This is because water takes up less space than ice.

You will need
2 cups of ice

Did You Know?
Ice cubes melt when you put them in a drink. Even if the drink has come from the refrigerator, it will not be cold enough to stop the ice from melting. Because the drink is a liquid, you know it is warmer than freezing point. When the temperature rises above freezing point, ice starts to melt.

Boiling

Boiling changes liquid water to gas. The molecules in a gas are far apart and free to move about. Water turns to gas at 100°C (212°F). This is called the boiling point. Boiling is part of the process of turning salty sea-water into drinking water. This process is called distillation.

Making distilled water
Salty sea-water is distilled thousands of gallons at a time in special distillation plants. You can make a small amount of distilled water in a kitchen.

1. Place a saucepan of water on the hob. Stir in lots of salt. Taste the water to make sure it is very salty.

2. Put a tight-fitting lid on the pan. Bring the water to the boil.

3. Using oven gloves, carefully lift off the lid. Turn it upside-down. As the cold air hits the lid, the steam cools down. It then turns into small drops of water. This is called condensation. Pour this water into a bowl carefully. Put the lid back on the saucepan of boiling water.

4. Continue until you have enough water in the bowl to taste. The water will not taste of salt at all. Be sure the water has cooled down before you taste it!

You will need
a saucepan with a
  tight-fitting lid
water
salt
oven gloves
a heatproof bowl

Cooking by Boiling

For thousands of years people have cooked food by boiling it. They do this because boiling softens food and kills harmful bacteria. Boiling also "kills" the cells in food.

"Killing" a carrot

This experiment will show you the difference between the cells of a living carrot and a carrot that has been boiled.

1. Cut a big, thick carrot into two pieces, each about 5cm (2 in) long. The pieces need to have flat ends. Cut a hole in the top of each piece.

2. Boil one piece for 10 minutes.

3. Carefully drain the carrot. When it is cool, stand it upright in the bowl with the cut hole on top.

4. Place the uncooked carrot upright in the bowl with the cut hole on top.

5. Pour enough water into the bowl to come 5mm (¼in) up each piece. Put a teaspoon of sugar in each hole. Leave the carrots to stand. After about 15 minutes, you should find the cavity in the uncooked carrot full of water and sugar. The sugar in the cooked carrot will be dry. This is because the water could pass up through the living cells in the uncooked carrot. It cannot pass through the dead cells in the cooked piece.

You will need
a carrot
a knife
a saucepan with lid
water
a drainer or slotted spoon
a small flat bowl
sugar

Did You Know?
The process of water passing through living cells is called osmosis. Here is another example of osmosis: Put a handful of raisins in a bowl. Pour some hot water over them. After about 30 minutes, the raisins will be much plumper and larger. There will also be less water in the bowl. The water will have passed into the raisins through the skin by osmosis.

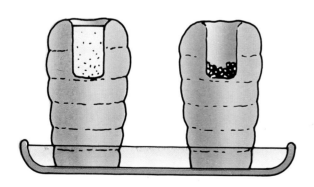

Dissolving

The salt in the experiment on page 12 seemed to vanish when you added it to the water. When you stir sugar into tea, it seems to disappear too. But if you taste the tea, you can tell the sugar is still there. This is because sugar dissolves in liquid.

Will it dissolve?
Not all substances dissolve. This experiment will show you that some substances dissolve and others do not. Do not empty the glasses when you have finished. You can use them for the next experiment.

Record your results in the notebook.

You will need
a notebook
a pencil
4 glasses
a spoon
salt
flour
dried herbs
bicarbonate of soda

1. Fill four glasses with water.

2. Stir salt into one glass. Did it dissolve?

3. Stir flour into one glass. Did it dissolve?

4. Stir dried herbs into one glass. Did they dissolve?

5. Stir bicarbonate of soda into one glass. Did it dissolve?

Did You Know?
A substance that dissolves in liquid is called a solute. The liquid is called a solvent. Together a solute and solvent make a solution.

Filtering

Filtering removes undissolved substances from liquid. The water from your tap has been filtered to clean it before it gets to your home.

Filtering liquid

A filter strains undissolved substances from liquid. When liquid is poured through the filter, anything that has not dissolved will remain in the filter.

1. Place a kitchen towel over a bowl.

2. Pour some water with salt mixed in it through the kitchen towel into the bowl. Is there any salt left on the paper?

3. Pour some water with flour mixed in it through another kitchen towel into the bowl. Is there any flour left on the paper?

4. Repeat these steps with the other ingredients.

Which ingredients did not dissolve?

You can tell that salt is in a solution even though you cannot see it. Tasting it is one way. There is another way, too. Leave a bowl of salt water in the sun. The water will evaporate and the salt will be left in the bottom of the bowl.

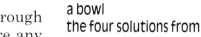

You will need
a sheet of paper
a pencil
4 kitchen towels
a bowl
the four solutions from
the previous experiment

Suspensions

Have you ever shaken a bottle of French-style salad dressing? At first, the oil and vinegar will be mixed together. Then, after a few minutes, they will separate into layers. This is an example of a suspension. In a suspension, the solute and solvent separate.

Making suspensions

This experiment will show you the difference between a suspension and a solution.

You will need
a spoon
a mug
instant coffee
water
a glass
powdered cocoa
milk

1. Place a spoonful of instant coffee in the bottom of a mug. Add some hot water and stir. Has the coffee dissolved? Does the coffee stay dissolved, or does it separate after 15 minutes?

2. Place a spoonful of powdered cocoa in the bottom of a glass. Very slowly pour in some cold milk. Stir quickly while you add the milk. Has the cocoa dissolved? Does the cocoa stay dissolved, or does it separate after 15 minutes?

Which is the suspension? The coffee or the cocoa?

Mixing Oil and Vinegar

If you put oil and vinegar in a jar with a lid and shake it, you can see that they separate. But, if you add an egg yolk, they can be beaten together. The mixture is then called an emulsion. The egg yolk is the emulsifier. The egg yolk coats each droplet of oil so it does not separate from the liquid.

Making mayonnaise

Mayonnaise is an emulsion. Make some to put on your sandwich or salad. Be sure to add the oil very slowly. If the oil is added too fast, the oil and vinegar will separate.

1. Mix together the egg yolk, all the dry ingredients and the vinegar.

2. Measure 150 ml (5 fl oz) of vegetable oil into a measuring jug.

3. With one hand beat the egg yolk mixture with a wooden spoon or wire whisk. With your other hand, dip a teaspoon into the oil. Slowly drip oil off the spoon drop by drop into the egg yolk mixture. Beat the egg yolk mixture as fast as you can while you add the oil. You may find it easier to ask a friend to drop in the oil while you beat the mixture.

4. Once the mixture begins to thicken, you can add the oil in a slow, steady stream. Continue beating until you have added all the oil.

5. You can use the mayonnaise for sandwiches and salads. Keep it in the refrigerator in a covered container. It will last for one week.

You will need

1 egg yolk
½ teaspoon mustard
a pinch of salt
a pinch of black pepper
a pinch of sugar
1 tablespoon vinegar
150 ml (5 fl oz) vegetable oil
a bowl
a wooden spoon or wire whisk
a teaspoon

Carbon Dioxide

You will need
2 small bowls
a spoon
bicarbonate of soda
water
vinegar
cling film

When you open a fizzy drink bottle, you will hear a "whish" sound and see lots of bubbles. They are caused by the carbon dioxide in the bottle. Carbon dioxide is a gas. Do you burp after you drink a fizzy drink? This is because you swallowed some of the carbon dioxide and it is escaping from your stomach.

Making carbon dioxide
Carbon dioxide is formed by combining an acid with a carbonate. Acids are a type of chemical that are usually sour-tasting. Vinegar and lemon juice are both acids. Carbonates contain both carbon and oxygen. Bicarbonate of soda is a carbonate.

1. Put 1 tablespoon of bicarbonate of soda into each of the bowls.

2. Stir 1 tablespoon of water into one bowl. Stir 1 tablespoon of vinegar into the other.

Both mixtures will turn white. Which one fizzes and has lots of bubbles? It should be the bowl with the vinegar. You have created carbon dioxide in this bowl.

Do the experiment again. This time loosely cover each bowl with cling film after you add the liquid. The cling film on the bowl with the vinegar will bulge up. The bulge is created by the carbon dioxide gas in the bowl.

Did You Know?
When carbon dioxide is added to a drink to make it fizzy, the process is called carbonation. Some mineral water comes from springs with carbon dioxide already present naturally.

Carbon Dioxide in Action

Because carbon dioxide is a gas, it is very light. Carbon dioxide is lighter than water, so it rises in water. When the gas gets to the water's surface, it floats out into the atmosphere.

Making mothballs dance
This experiment shows how carbon dioxide rises in liquid.

1. Place an empty coffee jar in the sink. Fill it three-quarters full of water. Stir in 14 tablespoons of vinegar.

2. Quickly stir in ½ tablespoon of bicarbonate of soda.

3. While the water is still fizzing, drop in three mothballs. The mothballs will sink to the bottom.

You will need
a large clean coffee jar
  (as tall as possible)
water
vinegar
bicarbonate of soda
mothballs

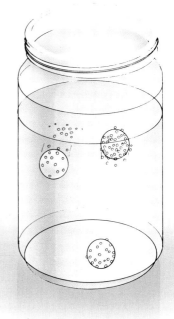

After about ten seconds, the mothballs will be covered with lots of little bubbles. These are bubbles of carbon dioxide.

When there are enough bubbles on each mothball, the mothball will float to the surface. When it reaches the surface, the carbon dioxide dissolves in the air at the top. The mothball sinks back down. As more carbon dioxide bubbles form, the mothball will dance back up again.

Starches

Starch is a food substance made by plants. Your body converts starches into energy. The only way you can get any starches is by eating foods that come from plants.

You will need

iodine
water
a small bowl
  (to mix iodine solution)
4 small plates
bacon
flour
a potato slice
cooked rice
an eye dropper

Finding the starches

When iodine touches food containing starch, it quickly changes colour. It turns from yellowy-orange to a very dark mauve. This simple experiment will help you find out which foods contain a lot of starch.

1. Make a solution of 25 ml (1 fl oz) of water and several drops of iodine. It will be yellow.

2. Put a piece of bacon on a small plate.

3. Put some flour on a small plate.

4. Put the slice of potato on a small plate.

5. Put the rice on a small plate.

6. Add a few drops of the iodine solution to each type of food. Which ones turn mauve?

The piece of bacon should have been the only food not to turn mauve. Bacon comes from an animal. It does not contain starch. If you do not have the foods suggested above, try this experiment with any other foods.

You can buy small amounts of iodine at a chemist. Use it carefully. It can make a yellow stain on your fingers.

Enzymes

Many of the foods you eat contain starch. In your body there are small protein molecules called enzymes. Enzymes help, or speed up, other chemical reactions. Some help break down starch.

1. Make a thin paste of flour and water in a bowl. It will be white.

2. Add a drop of iodine. The paste will turn dark mauve. This happens because flour is mostly starch.

3. Add a small amount of biological washing liquid and mix together well. Set the mixture aside. What happens after about 15 minutes? The mixture starts to turn white again. The enzymes in the washing liquid have broken down the starches.

You will need
flour
water
a bowl
a spoon
an eye dropper
iodine
biological washing liquid, the kind that contains enzymes

Did You Know?
The saliva in your mouth contains enzymes. See how it breaks down starch. Mash a piece of banana lightly. Spit on part of the banana. After about 30 minutes, the banana under the saliva will be soft and mushy.

Acids at Work

Acids are a type of chemical. Lemon juice and vinegar are two acids found in the kitchen. Acids can have strong reactions when combined with other substances. This experiment shows how acid reacts with calcium.

Acids destroy calcium

Calcium is one of the most important minerals in your body. Your body uses calcium to make strong bones and healthy teeth.

This experiment uses an eggshell. Eggshells contain a lot of calcium.

You will need

1 egg
2 dishes
malt vinegar

1. Crack an egg. Put the yolk and white in a dish and set aside. (You can use the yolk for the project on page 17)

2. Break the eggshell up into tiny pieces and put it in a small dish.

3. Pour in enough malt vinegar to cover the eggshell. Do not cover the dish.

After about three days, the vinegar will start to dissolve the eggshell. After a week, all that will be left is a thin membrane from the inside of the shell.

Did You Know?

Acids also affect your teeth. The enamel on your teeth is made of calcium. Tooth decay is caused by bacteria. The bacteria live off the sugar in your food. After the bacteria eats sugar, it produces acid. This acid causes cavities.

Vitamin C

It is very important that you eat some vitamin C every day. Your body needs it so that cuts and bruises can heal quickly. The only way your body can get vitamin C is from food. When you eat food containing vitamin C, chemical reactions in your body help absorb the vitamin. Many fruits are a good source of vitamin C, or ascorbic acid, its other name.

Detecting vitamin C

This simple experiment will show you which fruits have a lot of vitamin C. When fruits are cut or bruised, they turn brown. You may have seen this happen when you bite an apple and put it down. This browning is caused by a reaction between enzymes in the fruit and in the air. Vitamin C delays this reaction. Fruits with large amounts of vitamin C take longer to turn brown.

1. Cut the three fruits in half and leave them for an hour.

2. Compare the time it takes each one to turn brown. The apple will probably start to turn brown first. The banana will probably be next. Both of these fruits are low in vitamin C. The orange is a citrus fruit. Citrus fruits, such as grapefruits and satsumas, contain large amounts of vitamin C.

You will need
1 orange
1 apple
1 banana
a plate
a knife

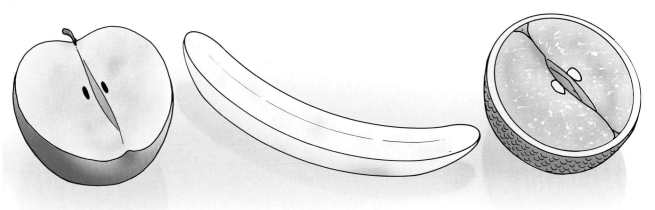

Hard and Soft Water

If you wash your hair when you stay in a different part of the country, you may find that you need more – or less – shampoo than usual. Different areas have different types of water. Some water is "hard" and some is "soft". Hard water contains extra minerals.

How soft is your water?
Soap used in soft water makes a thick lather. This simple experiment will show what type of water you have in your home.

You will need
2 jars with screw-top lids
distilled water
tap water
washing-up liquid

1.   Half-fill a screw-top jar with distilled water. Add a few drops of washing-up liquid. Put the lid on the jar tightly and shake it hard. Distilled water is soft water, so there should be lots of bubbles in the jar.

2.   Half-fill another jar with water from your tap. Add washing-up liquid and shake it well.

Are there a lot of bubbles or only a few? If there are lots, you have soft water. If there are only a few, you have hard water.

Another way to tell if you have hard or soft water is to look inside your electric kettle. If your water is hard, the element in the bottom of the kettle will look as if it has a coat of fur.

Salt Water

Have you ever been swimming in the sea on holiday? Was it easier to swim there than in a swimming pool? Sea-water is salty. Salt increases the density of water. More density means the water is able to support a solid object while it floats.

Floating eggs

This experiment shows how salt increases the density of water. It is also a good way to tell if an egg is really fresh.

1. Place an uncooked egg in its shell in a measuring jug filled with water. The egg will sink to the bottom. Remove the egg.

2. Stir in about 6 tablespoons of salt until the salt disappears. Add the same egg.

You will need
a measuring jug
water
1 egg
4 tablespoons salt

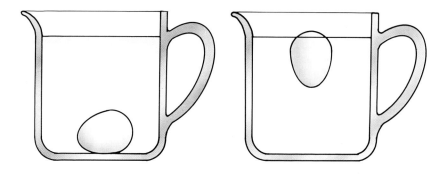

What happens to the egg? Does it float? It should float on the water's surface.

You can also use salt water to do the iceberg experiment on page 10. Do the experiment once with tap water and once with salt water. In which experiment do you think more of the ice cube will be floating above the water's surface?

Did You Know?
If an egg floats in fresh water, it is stale. Water inside an egg evaporates through the shell as the egg gets older. With less water, the egg is lighter, so it floats.

Ethylene Gas

Many fruits are picked and shipped to markets and shops before they are fully ripe. If you have some underripe fruit, it is easy to use simple chemistry to speed up the ripening process.

Ripening a banana

Fruits naturally produce a gas called ethylene. This gas helps the ripening process. Apples produce more ethylene gas than most fruit. If you combine an apple and an underripe fruit, the ethylene gas from the apple will help the other fruit ripen more quickly.

You will need
2 underripe bananas
an apple
a paper bag

1. Select two underripe bananas. They should be green and hard. (If you have trouble finding these, ask a local greengrocer to help you.)

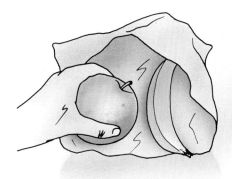  

2. Place one banana in a paper bag with an apple. Close the bag.

3. Place the other banana in an open place.

4. Check both bananas every day.

Which fruit is ripe first?

Pretty Flowers

Nothing can live without moisture. Plants draw up water through their roots and stem by osmosis.

Making a colourful bouquet

It is possible to make a bouquet of different coloured flowers even when you have only white flowers. This simple experiment shows how plants drink water through their stems.

1. Fill several coffee jars with water. Add a few drops of food colour to each jar. If you prefer, you can use just one colour.

2. Put a plain white flower or two in each jar.

3. Leave the flowers in the jars overnight. In the morning, you will see how the flowers have absorbed the coloured water up the stems and through the veins of the petals.

You will need

jars
liquid food colours
water
white flowers

Searching for Light

Plants always grow towards sunlight. If you position a plant with its leaves away from the light, after several days the leaves will be facing towards the light. This is because plants can make food only in the presence of sunlight. The process of making food is called photosynthesis.

Making a plant maze
This project will show you how "clever" plants are at finding light. Without sunlight, green plants are not able to live. A plant will wind its way through a dark passage to find a source of light.

You will need
a cardboard box with
  dividers
a knife
a seedling that grows
  quickly
water
newspapers or a black
  plastic bag
tape

1. Find a cardboard box with cardboard dividers. (You should be able to get one at a corner shop or off-licence.)

2. Carefully cut a hole about 75 cm (3 in) square in one end of the box.

3. Remove the dividers from the box. Carefully cut a series of smaller holes in each of the dividers. Plan the holes so they form a "route" for the plant to follow. This is the maze.

4. Water a small seedling in a pot. A sweet pea or bean seedling should grow quickly. Place it in one corner of the box.

5. Tightly cover the top of the box with a black plastic bag or several layers of newspaper. Tape the covering in position so that no sunlight comes in through the top.

6. Position the box so that the big hole in the side of the box faces the sunlight. After several days you will see the growing plant winding its way through the maze. Don't forget to water the plant a little every day. Untape the cover and water the plant quickly, then tape the cover back in position.

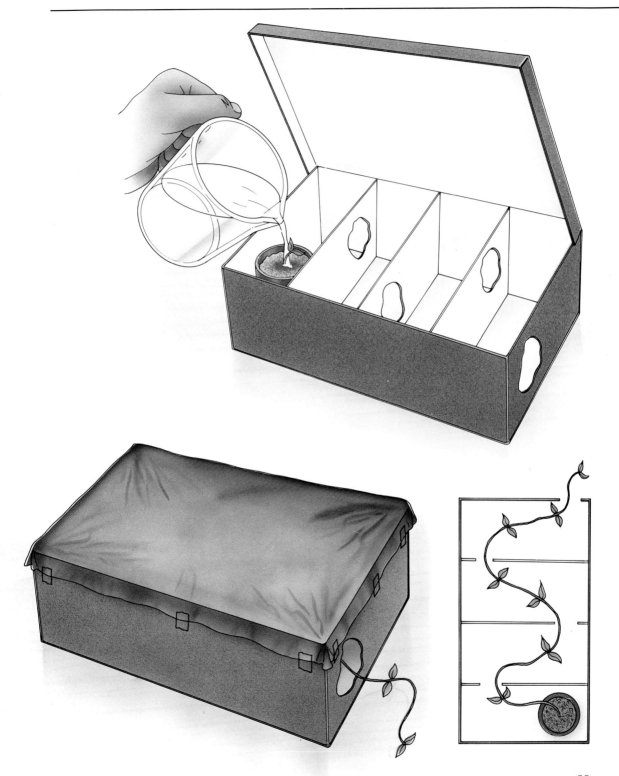

Healthy Eating

Your body uses many chemical reactions to turn the food you eat into energy. It also uses food to keep you healthy.

Eating lots of different foods is the best way to eat a healthy diet. Different types of foods are used for different things in your body.

Here are the major food groups and the foods that contain the most of each kind of nutrient:

Protein

Protein is essential for growth and to repair any bruised or injured parts of the body. Leftover protein is made into energy. Good sources are red meat, turkey, chicken, prawns, fish, beans, nuts, eggs, cheese and other dairy products.

Fat

Fat is necessary for energy. Good sources are dairy products like milk, cheese and butter. If you use oil in cooking or for making salad dressing, health experts recommend using oils from plants rather than animals. These include sunflower, corn and olive oils. Too much fat in your diet will make you overweight. It may also cause heart problems when you are older.

Carbohydrate

Carbohydrate is the major source of the body's energy. It is a form of starch. If you do not eat carbohydrates every day, you will be too tired to play or do sports. Good sources are bread, potatoes, rice, cereals and fruit.

Did You Know?

It is important to eat vegetable material that we cannot digest. Fruit, beans, peas, leafy vegetables and unrefined cereals all contain fibre. Fibre helps us digest the rest of our food, but contains no nutrients itself. A healthy diet always includes plenty of fibre.

Vitamins and minerals

These are what keep your bones and teeth strong. They make your hair shiny and your skin clear. Vitamins and minerals also keep your blood healthy. The best sources are fresh food. Fruit, vegetables, dairy products, meat and fish all contain lots of vitamins and minerals. Eating lots of different foods every day is a good way to get enough vitamins and minerals.

Water

You should drink a litre of water a day. Every cell in your body contains water. The cells need a constant supply. Your body can stay healthier longer without food than it can without water. In hot weather drink extra water.

32

How healthy is your diet?

Do you eat a variety of foods every day? Or, do you just eat your favourite food as often as you can?

What happens if you eat only fish fingers? It means your body is getting some protein, a little fat and some carbohydrates. You will not be eating fibre and you will not be getting many vitamins and minerals.

If you eat fish fingers twice a week, and other healthy foods for the other meals, you should get the food combinations you need.

Make a food chart like this for every day for a week. Fill it in after every meal. It will help you see how healthy your diet is.

Foods	Breakfast	Lunch	Dinner	Snacks
Protein	Bacon	Ham	Fish	Peanuts
Fat	Butter	Cheese	Butter	Crisps
Fibre	Wholemeal Toast	Bread	Broccoli and Grapes	Peanuts
Carbohydrate	Toast	Bread	Chips	Peanuts and Crisps
Vitamins + Minerals	Orange Juice	Apple	Grapes	Satsuma
Water	1 Glass	1 Glass	2 Glasses	Satsuma

Making Bread

Carbon dioxide is very important in baking. It makes bread rise. Yeast is a one-celled fungus. It makes carbon dioxide in bread dough. When yeast is combined with sugar and warm liquid, it multiplies very fast. As the yeast multiplies, it gives off carbon dioxide. This process is called fermentation. Fermentation is also used to make beer and wine.

Yeast in action

This project is done in two stages. The first stage shows yeast making carbon dioxide. The second stage shows how the carbon dioxide works in making bread. When you finish both stages, you will have 12 delicious rolls to serve with dinner.

Do not start this project unless you have about 2½ hours free. Read through all the steps before you begin.

Stage One

1. Combine 150 ml (5 fl oz) of boiling water and 150 ml (5 fl oz) of water from the tap in a heatproof measuring jug. You should have 300 ml (10 fl oz) of warm water. Stir in 1 teaspoon of sugar. Sprinkle the contents of one packet of dried yeast over the top. Stir once.

2. Set the measuring jug aside in a warm place. A sunny windowsill is ideal.

3. After about 5 minutes, bubbles will start to appear on the surface of the liquid. These are of carbon dioxide being made by the yeast.

Stage Two

4. In a large bowl, mix together 450 g (1 lb) of flour and 1 teaspoon of salt. Rub in 30 g (1 oz) of butter with your fingertips.

5. Pour the yeast water into the flour mixture. Be sure to add all the bubbles on the side of the jug. Use your hands to mix the flour and liquid together.

You will need

a measuring jug
a bowl
150 ml (5fl oz) boiling
  water
150 ml (5fl oz) tap water
1 teaspoon sugar
1 packet dried yeast
450 g (1 lb) flour
1 teaspoon salt
30 g (1 oz) butter
extra flour (for dusting)
a tea towel
a baking tray
an egg (optional)
oven gloves
a wire rack

6. Put the dough on a lightly floured work surface. Use the heels of your hands to knead the dough back and forth. Kneading distributes the carbon dioxide all through the dough. Continue kneading for about ten minutes. The dough will become smooth.

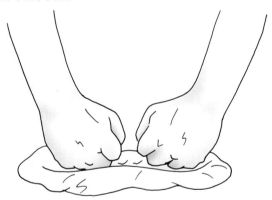

7. Put the dough back in the bowl. Cover the bowl with a clean tea towel. Set the bowl in a warm place for about 30 minutes. The size of the dough will double. This is caused by the carbon dioxide rising inside the dough. If the dough has not doubled in 30 minutes, leave it until it does.

8. Put the dough on a lightly floured work surface. Cut it in half with a knife. You will see lots of holes in the dough. These are pockets of carbon dioxide.

9. Knead the dough again for about five minutes.

10. Divide the dough into 12 equal-sized pieces. Roll each piece between your hands and shape it into a smooth ball. Place each ball of dough on a lightly floured baking tray. Leave them to rise for about 15 minutes.

11. Preheat the oven to 220°C/425°F/gas7.

12. Meanwhile, if you want a shiny finish on the rolls, make an egg glaze. Beat 1 egg with 1 tablespoon of water in a small bowl. Brush each piece of dough with the egg glaze.

13. Bake the rolls for 15 minutes. Using oven gloves, remove the baking tray from the oven carefully. Pick up one of the rolls and tap it on the bottom. If it sounds "hollow", the roll is cooked. Test another roll. If they do not sound hollow, return them to the oven for two more minutes. Test again. When the rolls are baked, transfer them to a wire rack to cool. Turn off the oven.

Flourless Baking

Baking usually uses flour. Flour is a starch. It helps to bind other ingredients together. But starch does not always have to be used. This project makes biscuits using ground almonds and sugar. You beat air into the mixture to make it light.

You will need

a mixing bowl
a wooden spoon
125 g (4 oz) butter
125 g (4 oz) caster sugar
125 g (4 oz) ground
  almonds
1 tablespoon ground
  cinnamon
a baking tray
oven gloves
a spatula
a wire rack

Making almond biscuits

1. Preheat the oven to 140°C/275°F/gas 1

2. In a bowl, mix together 125 g (4 oz) of caster sugar and 125 g (4 oz) of softened butter. Beat with a wooden spoon until the mixture is very light and fluffy. It will take a few minutes, so do not give up.

3. Fold in 125 g (4 oz) of ground almonds and 1 tablespoon of ground cinnamon.

4. Drop the mixture in 14 even-sized mounds on a large baking tray. Bake for 45-55 minutes, or until the biscuits are just turning brown on the edges.

5. Put on oven gloves. Take the biscuits from the oven carefully and leave them for 2 minutes. Use a spatula and very carefully transfer the biscuits to a wire rack to cool. They are very soft when they are warm. As they cool, they will become crisper.

Nobody likes tough meat. You can use chemistry to tenderise meat before you cook it.

Tenderising meat

You learned about enzymes that help digest starches on pages 20 and 21. Pineapple contains an enzyme that tenderises meat naturally. If you coat meat pieces with pineapple before cooking, the meat becomes tender when it is cooked.

1. Cut a pineapple in half and scoop out the flesh. Mash it with a fork.

2. Remove the skin from two chicken breasts. Cut each breast into four pieces.

3. Mix four of the chicken pieces with the pineapple in a bowl. Cover with cling film and place in the refrigerator for 15 minutes. Cover the remaining chicken pieces in a different bowl with cling film. Put them in the refrigerator.

4. Thread the chicken pieces with mashed pineapple on to a skewer. Add a mushroom between each piece. Heat the grill to high.

5. Make another kebab with the remaining chicken pieces and some mushrooms.

6. Grill the kebabs for 8-10 minutes until the chicken is cooked through. Turn the kebabs over every 2 minutes.

Which kebab is tenderer?

You will need
2 chicken breasts
a pineapple
a spoon
a knife
a fork
2 bowls
cling film
2 skewers
8 small button
  mushrooms

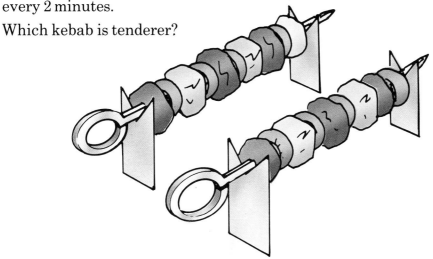

Moolds in the Air

Moulds are kinds of fungus that grow on food. They look like tiny bushes. They grow from invisible spores that are in the air. Most moulds are a sign that food is rotten. Some moulds, however, cause chemical reactions that are used to make certain foods, like some kinds of cheese. Moulds like a warm, damp atmosphere.

Making moulds

Moulds come in a variety of colours. Some are white or grey, and others are blue-green. See what different coloured moulds you can grow. After the moulds grow, throw the food away. *Do not eat it.*

You will need
a selection of uncooked foods
plastic sandwich bags

1. Assemble a selection of different types of uncooked foods. You can use whatever you want. Some good ones would be a slice of cheese, a rasher of unsmoked bacon, a piece of banana peel, a slice of bread, a spoonful of double cream, half a lemon.

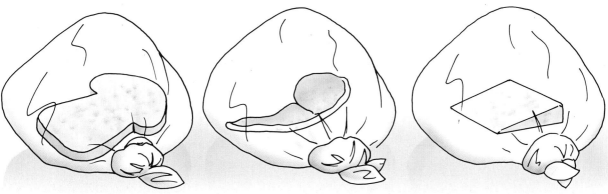

2. Put each type of food in its own small plastic sandwich bag. One by one, blow into each bag, then seal it tight. Try not to let any of the air escape.

3. Place the bags in a warm, dark place like a cupboard. After several days, a selection of moulds will start developing. How many different colours do you have?

40

Making Glue

Many foods, such as potatoes and flour, contain starch. Starches do not dissolve in liquids.

Making glue

This simple project takes advantage of the fact that starches do not dissolve at room temperature. You can make glue for sticking paper.

1. Put a large heaped spoonful of flour in a bowl. Use the spoon to push some of the flour towards the sides of the bowl. This will make a hollow "well" in the centre.

You will need
a large spoon
a bowl
flour
water

2. Slowly add a little water to the hollow. Stir to mix the flour and water. If you add too much water at once, the mixture will be lumpy.

3. Slowly stir in more water until the paste is smooth. If it is too thick, add a little more water. If the paste is too thin, put a little more flour in another bowl. Slowly stir the thin paste into the flour. Store your paste in a screw-top jar until you need it.

Safety Notes

The projects and experiments in this book are designed to show how certain principles of science work. Most of them are simple to do. Some of them should not be done without permission from an adult. These experiments are marked with this symbol:

It is a good idea to ask permission in any case. You should also make sure that an adult is available to answer any questions that you have.

Some projects are marked with the symbol: (A)

DO NOT TRY TO DO THESE UNLESS YOU HAVE AN ADULT
AVAILABLE TO HELP YOU.

Good scientists are very careful. They always protect themselves and other people. They listen to good advice. If you follow the rules given here, you should always stay safe.

Starting work
Before you begin, read the instructions. This will help you understand what must be done. Read the list of materials that you need. Collect everything on the list and put it in one place before you start. Some experiments need some preparation, such as cutting things out or measuring and weighing. Do this first. Remember to get permission if you need it.

Heat, fire and electricity
Some of the projects may involve the use of heat or a flame. Anything that is hot can burn you. Never play with fire, heat or electricity.

Remember that fire is always dangerous. Always ask an adult to help with experiments in which you need to use a cooker or the flame from a candle. Use only safety matches. Place all your materials so that you do not need to reach across a flame. Do not wear loose clothing that could accidentally get caught in the flame. Keep a pail or jug of water close by just in case.

If you are using electricity, always ask an adult to keep an eye on you. Remember that mains electricity can kill.

Sharp edges
Some of the projects may involve the use of scissors or knives. Objects with sharp edges are dangerous. Always ask an adult to help with these experiments. Get them to cut out things that you need for a project. Be very careful when opening tins or using mirrors.

Remember that glass breaks easily and broken glass has sharp edges. Most of the projects can be done using plastic jars and glasses. If you do break a glass, get someone to help clear it up immediately.

Chemicals

Some of the projects may involve the use of chemicals. All the chemicals used in this book are harmless household substances, but all chemicals should be treated with respect. Make sure that all containers of chemicals are labelled clearly. Keep them out of the reach of small children and inquisitive animals. Never mix chemical substances unless you are sure that you know what will happen. Some harmless chemicals can become dangerous when they are mixed together. Make sure that you dispose of your chemicals when you have finished the experiment. Wrap dry substances in old newspaper and throw them away. Pour liquids down the sink or an outside drain and flush them away thoroughly with plenty of clean water.

Tools and equipment

Tools such as hammers and nails or drills can cause injury. Always ask an adult for help if you need to use tools in an experiment. They can help you nail or glue things together or drill holes or cut things out.

General rules for safe science

* If in doubt, ask for help from an adult.
* Always wash your hands before you start and when you finish.
* Cover your work surface with old newspapers to protect it.
* Never do any experiment without careful planning. Never try an experiment just to see what will happen.
* You can collect useful objects such as empty containers, card or paper, pencils, etc, to help you in your experiments. Always make sure they are clean. Store them neatly in a convenient place.
* It is a good idea to keep a notebook of your experiments. Take notes after you have done an experiment. Your notes will be useful in the future. If you find that an experiment does not work, your notes will help you understand why. Then you can try the experiment again.
* Always clear everything up after you have finished your experiment. Put away any materials that are left and put any equipment that you have used back where it belongs. Throw away any rubbish.
* Keep dangerous objects and substances out of the reach of smaller children and animals.

Words to Remember

absorb incorporate one substance into another by chemical action

acid a sour substance

bacteria tiny organisms that grow all round you. You need a
  very strong microscope to see bacteria, even though they are
  everywhere – in the air and on all the food you eat. Some are harmful,
  some are not.

biological relating to biology

biology the study of life and all living things

carbohydrate one of the components of some foods. Starch and sugar
  are carbohydrates.When your body digests carbohydrates, they are
  turned into energy.

carbonation to put carbon dioxide in a liquid

chemical reaction a process which changes the chemical composition
  of a substance

condense to make denser or thicker. Condensed milk, for example,
  is thicker than ordinary milk.

density a measure of how thick, or compact, a substance is

distillation a process that removes impurities from liquid. The first
  step is to turn the liquid into vapour by heating it. The vapour is then
  cooled. When the vapour cools, it leaves behind the impurities.

emulsify to combine two ingredients which do not normally mix.
  Small drops of one liquid are suspended in the second liquid.
  When two ingredients are emulsified, they create an emulsion.

enzyme a protein that causes biochemical reactions to happen.
  (Biochemical is a combination of the words biology and chemistry.)

filter a device that collects objects suspended in liquid while letting
  the liquid pass through. A coffee filter, for example, collects the
  coffee grounds.

freeze to turn liquid into a solid. When frozen, the molecules have
  a definite shape and do not move.

gas an invisible collection of certain kinds of molecules that can
  move freely in all directions

iceberg giant pieces of ice that float in the sea. Some icebergs
  are several kilometres long.

knead to pound and stretch bread dough. Kneading distributes the gas given off by yeast throughout the dough. This is what makes bread light.

lather the frothy bubbles produced when soap and water are combined

liquid wet substances that are made of molecules that are able to move about.

melt to turn a solid substance back into a liquid, such as turning ice back to water

mineral an inorganic substance that does not come from a plant or animal. Minerals usually have to be extracted from the ground by mining.

molecule small particles of matter. Molecules are so tiny you can not see them. Even a single speck of dust contains millions of molecules.

mould small fungi that grow on plant and animal foods. Moulds usually look very fuzzy. Mould is often an indication that something is beginning to decay.

ripe when fruit and vegetables are ready to eat

protein a component of some foods. Your body needs protein for growth and to maintain all its functions.

saliva spit is the common name for saliva. The saliva in your mouth contains enzymes. These enzymes start to break down food when you chew it so your body can digest the food.

solute a substance that dissolves in liquid. Sugar, for example, is the solute in sweetened tea.

solution a liquid which has had another substance dissolved in it. Salt water, for example, is a solution because it has salt dissolved in the water.

suspension a liquid containing substances that have not dissolved

vapour what liquid becomes when it is heated. The molecules of a vapour are suspended in air. Steam is a vapour.

vegetarian a person who does not eat meat

vitamin a component of food that your body needs to help it grow and stay healthy

yeast a single-celled plant. Yeast is used in making bread and alcohol.

Books to Read

Usborne Introduction to Chemistry by Jane Chisholm Usborne Books 1983
Everyday Chemicals by Terry Jennings Oxford University Press 1984
Simple Chemistry by Neil Ardley Franklin Watts 1984
Simple Chemistry by John & Dorothy Paull Ladybird Books 1983
Longman Illustrated Dictionary of Chemistry Longman Books 1982
Fun with Science: Water by Brenda Walpole Kingfisher Books 1987
Turn on a Tap by Joy Richardson Hamish Hamilton 1988
Focus on Salt by David Lambert Wayland Books 1987
Salt by Richard Gibbs Wayland Books 1980
Salt by Valerie Pitt Franklin Watts 1974
Heat & Temperature by M Merigot Burke Books 1983
Energy for Life by Ed Catherall Wayland Books 1982
Making Bread by Ruth Thompson Franklin Watts 1986
Beans and Pulses by Susanna Miller Wayland Books 1989
Eggs by Dorothy Turner Wayland Books 1988
The Science Book by Sara Stein Heinemann 1979
The All Year Round series by Kathleen Edwards Macdonald 1987
Why Things Are general editor: Lesley Firth Kingfisher Books 1989
Beginning to Learn about Science by Richard L Allington PhD and Kathleen
  Krull Blackwell Raintree Ltd 1983
Simple Science Experiments by Eiji and Masako Orii Gareth Stevens 1989
Longman Illustrated Science Dictionary 1981
Science for Life by Bishop, Maddocks and Scott Collins Educational 1984
Life on Earth by Linda Gamlin Gloucester Press 1988
Fire and Water by Robin Kerrod Cherrytree Press 1988

Index

Acid 18, 22

Bacteria 13, 22
Body 20, 21, 22, 23, 30-31, 32, 33
Boiling 12, 13

Calcium 22
Carbohydrate 31, 33
Carbonate 18
Carbonation 18
Carbon dioxide 18, 19, 34-36
Cells 13
Citrus fruit 23
Cold 9, 11
Condensation 12

Density 25
Diet 30, 33
Digestion 21
Dissolving 14, 15
Distillation 12

Emulsifier 17
Emulsion 17
Energy 20, 30-31
Enzyme 21, 23, 39
Ethylene gas 26
Evaporation 15, 25

Fat 31, 33
Fermentation 34
Fibre 32, 33
Filtering 15
Food 13, 20, 21, 23, 30-33, 41
Freezing 8-9, 10

Gas 7, 12, 15, 18, 19, 26
  Ethylene gas 26

Heat 11, 12, 13

Ice 8, 9, 10, 11, 25

Kneading 36

Liquid 7, 8, 11, 12, 14, 15, 17, 19, 41

Melting 11
Minerals 24, 32, 33
Molecule 8, 11, 12, 21
Moulds 40

Nutrients 30

Osmosis 13, 27

Photosynthesis 28
Plants 20, 27, 28
Protein 30, 33

Ripening 26

Saliva 21
Salt 12, 15, 25
Solid 8, 11, 25
Solute 14, 16
Solution 14, 15, 16
Solvent 14, 16
Starch 20, 21, 31, 38, 41
Steam 12
Sunlight 28
Suspension 16

Temperature 11, 12, 13, 41
Tenderising 39

Vapour 15
Vitamin C 23
Vitamins 32, 33

Water 7, 8, 9, 10, 12, 13, 15, 19, 24, 25,
    27, 32
  Distilled water 12
  Hard water 24
  Salt water 12, 25
  Sea water 25
  Soft water 24

Yeast 34-35